I0440774

This book is dedicated to my third born son, Bradley Michael. It was on our trip to Rocky Mountain National Park that he decided to stay in Colorado and live there.

A Close Up Look at

Rocky Mountain National

Park

By Josie Zayac

Rocky Mountain National Park is the greatest place to go.

Even in the summer you are bound to see some snow.

Take a close look.
What do you see?

A little white flower, called mariposa lily.

Take a close look.
look.
What do you see?

The golden banner.

Related to the pea.

Take a close look.
What do you see?

Lichen grows on a rock, log, or tree.

Take a close look.
What do you see?

It's a
little
chippy.

(chipmunk)

Take a close look.
What do you see?
Could it be the branch of a
tree?

NO! It's an elk getting dinner for free.

Take a close look.
What do you see?

It's Clark's
nutcracker
who eats
pine seeds.

Take a close look.
What do you see?

It's the
leaves of
an aspen
tree.

Take a close look.
What do you see?

All kinds of
wildflowers,
so delightful
to see.

Take a close look. What do you see?

Rushing water is thrilling to me!

Take a close look.
What do you see?

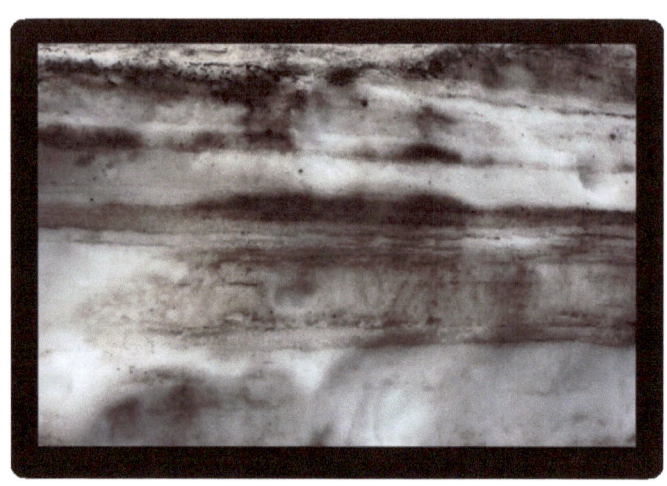

Layers of snow that's all dirty.

The mountains are high,
The air is so cold.
Even in summer,
The Rockies have snow.

Take a close look.
What do you see?

The powerful wind makes a twisted tree.

Take a close look.
What do
you see?

It's a begging burro, headed straight for me!

Take a close look.
What do you see?
The Rocky Mountains'
wildlife and trees.

Go out and explore.

Breathe the fresh air.

Take care of our park.

And show that you care.

Facts about Rocky Mountain National Park, Colorado

- Located in Colorado, the world's longest mountain barrier
- Founded on January 26, 1915
- Has 72 peaks over 12,000 feet high
- Covers 415 square miles, which is 265,828 acres
- The Continental Divide runs through the center of the park
- Has glaciers, lakes, waterfalls,and alpine tundra,
- Trees include pines and aspen
- Animals include elk, mule deer, moose, sheep, pika, and pine marten

Look for other National Park books by Dr. Josie Zayac

- A Close Up Look at Bryce Canyon National Park
- A Close Up Look at Crater Lake National Park
- A Close Up Look at Cuyahoga Valley National Park
- A Close Up Look at Joshua Tree National Park
- A Close Up Look at Redwood National and State Parks
- A Close Up Look at Rocky Mountain National Park
- A Close Up Look at Sequoia National Park
- A Close Up Look at Theodore Roosevelt National Park
- A Close Up Look at Zion National Park

www.ingramcontent.com/pod-product-compliance
Lightning Source LLC
Chambersburg PA
CBHW050930290526
45792CB00002B/953